I0198888

In this series –

RUMI READINGS
FOR
YOUTH

RUMI READINGS
FOR
YOUTH

JALALUDDIN RUMI

The Scheherazade Foundation

The Scheherazade Foundation CIC
85 Great Portland Street
London
W1W 7LT
United Kingdom
www.SF.Charity
info@SF.Charity

First published by The Scheherazade Foundation CIC, 2025

RUMI READINGS FOR YOUTH

© The Scheherazade Foundation

The Scheherazade Foundation asserts the right to be identified as the Author of the Work in accordance with the Copyright, Designs and Patents Act 1988.

A CIP catalogue record for this title is available from the British Library.

ISBN 978-1-915311-82-5

All rights reserved. No part of this publication may be reproduced, stored in a retrieval system, or transmitted, in any form or by any means, electronic, mechanical, photocopying, recording or otherwise, without the prior written permission of the publisher.

This book is sold subject to the condition that it shall not, by way of trade or otherwise, be lent, re-sold, hired out or otherwise circulated without the publisher's prior consent in any form of binding or cover other than that in which it is published and without a similar condition including this condition being imposed on the subsequent purchaser.

Introduction

Jalaluddin Rumi was born in Balkh, Afghanistan, in the year 1207, and died in Konya, Turkey, in 1273.

During the sixty-six years spanning this pair of dates, he produced a range of extraordinary work in Persian which, today, is classed as 'Sufi Mysticism'.

In the seven and a half centuries since his death, Rumi's corpus, which includes *The Masnavi* and *Fihi Ma Fihi*, has been circulated widely across the Near East, the Arab world, and Central Asia.

Generations of students continue to commit selections of the 60,000 verses to heart, and allow Rumi's way of thought to permeate through all areas of their lives.

Although Orientalists venturing eastward from Europe in the 1700s occasionally made note of Sufi Mysticism, they tended to witness it through the more theatrical frills – such as 'whirling dervishes' – rather than through a deep appreciation of the texts.

It wasn't until the close of the nineteenth century that the first wholescale translations of Rumi's written work began to appear in Europe.

Even then, they remained very much the purview of a few academics, whose translations were – even for the time – laden with indescribably floral and cumbersome prose.

Although in the Occident, students would find themselves scrutinizing Rumi's corpus, it wasn't until more recently that accessible appreciations of his work became available.

A few years before his death, I asked my father – the Sufi scholar and thinker Idries Shah – for his thoughts on Rumi's legacy in the West.

Sitting in his favourite chair, a porcelain cup of green tea in hand, he looked at me hard.

'I never cease to be amazed,' he said.

'Amazed by what?'

'By the way people don't take what's perfectly packaged, and ready and waiting for them, but rather obsess with something else.'

'With what?'

'With endless and nonsensical trimmings, trappings, and paraphernalia.'

My father sipped his tea.

After a moment of silent thought, he continued:

'Read Rumi in the original Persian,' he said, 'and so delicate are the verses that you have tears rolling down your cheeks. Yet here in the West, it's served up as something submerged in a thick, glutinous gravy, so much so that its utterly inedible.'

I reminded my father that a series of publications had recently found their way to press – publications that presented Rumi's couplets in an utterly new way.

Stripped bare of what my father had referred to as 'gravy', they were light.

Indeed, they were lighter than light.

My father rolled his eyes at the thought.

'In any other place, and at any other time,' he said, 'people would be up in arms. Or, if they weren't, they'd be laughing until their sides split. Imagine it – Western poets with absolutely no knowledge of the original Persian text touting new, bestselling editions of Rumi's work! It's what we call "The Soup of the Soup of the Soup".'

In the years since my father's death, Occidental society has been flooded with all things Rumi.

Couplets ascribed to him are read solemnly at weddings across the United States, Europe, and beyond.

Wisdom drawn from his poetry is tattooed daily over the backs and limbs of Hollywood A-listers.

But the precious words uttered at weddings, tattooed into skin, and quoted in abundance, hold little or no bearing to the original verses of Jalaluddin Rumi.

So, there it is…

The great Sufi Master's wisdom available:

(a) in a form that's unreadable because it's all covered in glutinous gravy, or

(b) in another form that's completely distorted – the Soup of the Soup of the Soup.

One thing that *is* evident is that the West can benefit enormously from a clean, clear rendition of Rumi's thinking – as the East has done over the last seven hundred years.

For this reason, we have commissioned entirely new translations, gleaned in particular from *The Masnavi*. Selected and translated by native Persian-speaking scholars, the emphasis has been on maintaining the lightness of Rumi's poetry.

In an age of relentless speed and digital overload, and so as to allow the work to be accessed by those who may benefit from it most, we have arranged a series of bite-sized morsels by way of theme.

We encourage you to do what students, scholars, and ordinary people have done across the East for centuries...

To pick a single couplet, or a handful – and to read them over and over, allowing them to seed themselves in your mind.

Little by little, having taken root, they will blossom and bear fruit.

Tahir Shah

How to Use This Book

Rumi Readings for Youth

This book is for the restless, the searching, the uncertain, the bold.

It is for those at the beginning – or what *feels* like the beginning – those asking big questions and facing new choices.

It is for those growing, becoming, changing – and wondering what any of it means.

Rumi Readings for Youth gathers one hundred quotes from *The Masnavi* and other works by the great Sufi master, translated directly from the original Persian by The Scheherazade Foundation. These verses have been selected to speak to the themes of youth: energy, desire, identity, confusion, purpose, rebellion, friendship, responsibility, imagination.

Rumi understood youth not as a phase to survive, but as a power to be awakened.

He did not write down to the young. He wrote **into** them – with clarity, compassion, and challenge.

Let this book be a companion – something to return to, especially when the road ahead feels unclear.

No Need to 'Figure It Out'

You don't need to be on a spiritual path to use this book.
You don't need to understand Persian poetry.
You don't need to believe anything at all.

All you need is a little curiosity – and a willingness to pause now and then.

The quotes are arranged in ten themed parts.
But you can read them however you like:
Start from the beginning. Open at random. Follow a feeling. Ask a question and see what appears.

There is no one right way.

Read One Line at a Time

Try reading a single quote. Slowly.
Not for information – but for reflection.

Ask yourself:

- What does this remind me of?
- What part of me is it speaking to?
- What would it mean if this were true?

You might feel nothing at first. Or you might feel something stir.

That's enough. Let the quote work in the background.

Come back to it later. Or don't. Trust your own rhythm.

Journal, Reflect, Explore

If you like writing, try responding to the quotes.

You can free-write, answer questions, or just note what the quote brings up.

Ask questions. Let it prompt memories. Or just write what you're feeling.

For When You Feel Lost

Some days are confusing. Some are overwhelming.
Some are just... blank.

This book can meet you in all of them.

Rumi doesn't offer easy answers – but he does offer companionship. He reminds you that not knowing is part of becoming. That confusion is a form of honesty. That you're not the only one wondering where you're going.

Let the words sit with you when everything else is loud.

Let them be a breath when the world speeds up.

Share If You Want

If a quote speaks to you, send it to someone. A friend. A sibling. A mentor.
Let it be a bridge – between what you're feeling and what you want to say.

You might be surprised how many people are carrying the same questions, the same hopes, the same heaviness.

Let the words speak for you.

Let them open something real.

You Are Already Enough

Rumi never saw young people as unfinished.
He saw them as luminous – powerful, brave, and full of possibility.

Not perfect. Not complete. But already *enough* to begin.

He writes in this volume:
'The period of youth, like a green and bountiful garden, produces fruit and crops in abundance.'

Let this book remind you of your own abundance.
Let it challenge you to see what's inside you – and who you're becoming.

You don't have to be anyone else.
You just have to be *yourself*, with your eyes open.

Part 1

Characteristics of Youth

1

When there is strength,
there is health,
and the heart has vigour and power.

2

The period of youth,
like a green and bountiful garden,
produces fruit and crops in abundance.

3

The springs of vitality and longing surge,
causing physical foundation to blossom.

4

The house is constructed with strong materials
and has a good, high roof.
Its foundations are stable,
and free from any contamination.

5

The reflection that the young see in the mirror is what older people perceive in shapeless clay.

6

In your youth, you were both satisfied and fulfilled;
you pursued wealth,
yet had inherent value.

7

Projectiles soar through the air;
the hidden cower out of view;
innumerable weathered arrows
impact the young.

8

Fortunate is the individual
who appreciates and cherishes their days of youth,
and fulfils their obligations.

9

Awake, for it is the essence,
the entire world and the vitality of youth;
the sun has ascended:
witness its brilliance!

10

We are romantically entwined,
lacking compassion, and poor;
encompassing childhood, youth, and old age.
As when sulphur and dry wood are combined,
we are ignited by the force and power of love.

Part 2

Youth &
Seizing Opportunity

11

Moses asked,
'O Lord, you have considered it,
but why have You caused it to become barren once more?'
God replied,
'I know that your question is not driven by denial,
negligence, or whim.
Otherwise, I would have reprimanded
and admonished you for asking it.'

12

Disregard the allure of the palace;
pull down the physical structure.
The treasure lies within the ruins.
He who gets drunk, finds joy,
even knowing that this leads to destruction.

13

Do not ask after our well-being,
or the specifics of our current condition.
For one who has transcended the understanding
of their own essence,
the method or manner in which it is achieved
becomes insignificant.
The wine of the mournful is depleted,
and we find greater contentment in our own libations.
Direct your attention to those who are trapped in sadness,
and give them your drink.
The wine may redden the features of the sorrowful,
but we find satisfaction
in the natural colour of our own face,
and our cheerful disposition.

14

I will suffer human mortality again
to ascend to the realm of angels,
adorned with wings and bestowed with higher status.
To avoid chaos, I must also flee from the kingdom;
'Everything will be destroyed except for His Face.'
Once more, I shall willingly relinquish my position
in the kingdom to become something
beyond the realm of imagination.

15

Make effort in this period
to free yourself from the limitations of time,
before the moment when time
ceases to have any meaning.

16

Each breath in brings us fresh life,
even as we remain oblivious to its power of rejuvenation
occurring within the realm of reality.
Life, like a ceaseless current, is in perpetual motion;
it only appears to endure within the physical form.

17

The soul's journey is unaffected by temporal
or spatial constraints;
may our physical bodies draw wisdom from this voyage.

18

We consistently embody a state of freshness,
youthfulness and delicacy,
always new, sweet, smiling and elegant.
To us, a hundred years is indistinguishable
from a single hour,
as the concept of time is meaningless.

19

Regardless of the duration of the voyage,
the heart remains unaware of the true sources
of delight and inspiration.
The body possesses characteristics of length and brevity,
but the journey of the soul is distinct and separate.

20

To discover a concealed birthplace,
you must relinquish the slumber of earthly cravings,
like a radiant celestial body set against
the darkness of night.

Part 3

Youth &
the Passage of Time

21

O cup-bearer, when you yourself get drunk,
beat yourself before me;
forget the future and release the obligations
of tomorrow.

22

Every variation originates in the concept of time;
those who transcend time are free from all such variations.

23

A true Sufi is one who resides in the present moment,
O companion;
speaking of 'tomorrow' is not part of their path.

24

If you harbour hatred for every injury,
you will find yourself devoid of refinement
and self-reflection.
Exercising patience is a valuable virtue,
my brother.
By being patient, you can achieve a state of purity
and liberation from this enduring affliction.

25

People of refinement are free from any
unpleasant scent or colour;
they are able to perceive virtue instantly at every moment.

26

A Sufi is said to embody the present moment,
yet the truly enlightened transcends the constraints
of time and societal norms.
Their state relies on determination and purpose,
sustained by the vitality of a Christ-like spirit.

27

Awareness arises from our recollection
of prior experiences;
past and future act as barriers to understanding God.
Burn both with fire;
for how much longer will you remain attached to them,
like a fragile stem of a plant?

28

Do not passively observe and wait on this journey;
I assure you,
there is no death more terrible than waiting.

29

Exercise patience and keep your focus on the door;
those who wait with anticipation
will seize both opportunities and fate.

30

The inhabitants of this world are universally confined,
anticipating their death in this impermanent dwelling.
Except for a select few, every one
will be restricted tomorrow;
those still bound within their physical form
will not be able to break free
from their heavenly confinement.

Part 4
Youth & Desire

31

O rulers, we have conquered the external foe,
yet a more formidable adversary still resides within us.

32

Reason is a noble and enlightened guide,
yet the obscured Self often overcomes it.
Reason is a stranger within one's own house,
while ignorance stands guard at the door like a lion.

33

A soul cannot attain goodness
without enduring the transformative power of fire.
Just as iron must be forged to glow
as brightly as a burning ember.
When it achieves self-sufficiency,
it transforms into a pillar of strength;
yet once the burden is lifted,
even the donkey may kick out in defiance.

34

If you engage in self-reflection,
act in a contrary manner to the advice it provides,
as it may deceive.

35

We have news,
but you remain completely unaware;
a heart filled with envy is nothing but blood,
and you remain oblivious.
You are like a camel train carrying goods to the Kaaba.
But the reason for your absence from the journey
is not due to a lack of a donkey,
but a deliberate choice not to set off,
much like a donkey itself.

36

The sun's rays lit up the wall;
borrowed light gently caressed its surface.
What can you truly attach to a mere stone,
O virtuous one?
Seek instead the eternal and
enduring source of illumination.

37

The thorn maintains its shape
regardless of the direction in which it is pulled.
Pain can be felt even in Paradise,
and its impact is hard to avoid.
Burn the thorn with the flame of renouncing desire,
and seek the support of a righteous companion.

38

O Lord,
this act of generosity exceeds our own efforts;
your hidden benevolence is what truly becomes us.

39

Humans yearn for winter during hot summer months.
Yet when finally winter comes
they often forget their previous desire for its arrival.

40

Even if the vast expanse of the world's oceans
were completely depleted,
the intense longing of that person's spirit
would still remain unsatisfied.

Part 5
Youth & Identity

41

The person who lacks self-awareness
due to behaviour of excess
finds themself in a state of insufficiency.

42

The seeker will ultimately find what they are looking for,
regardless of how quickly they search.
Seek consistently and diligently, with both hands,
as the search itself can become a guide on the journey.

43

Whenever you benefit from an act of kindness,
try to identify the source of that goodness.
These actions come from a deep well.
Do not focus on individual elements;
instead, turn your attention to the whole.

44

A person devalues themselves,
despite their inherent worth,
and becomes confined to a lowly state.
What is the cause of their confusion?
Why do they choose to align with harmfulness,
when there are so many better alternatives?

45

The wind serves as a channel for Solomon,
the sea speaks to Moses,
the moon becomes a symbol for Ahmad,
and the fire transforms into a rose for Abraham.
Korah[1] is consumed by the earth, like a snake,
while the dust of Hanana[2] brings salvation.

---

1 Mentioned in the Old Testament and Qur'an, who led a rebellion against
Moses.
2 In certain Christian traditions, collected from the tombs of saints for healing
purposes.

46

Hundreds of thousands of shallow people gathered,
forming concentric circles around one another.
The dragon, feeling disheartened by the cold,
was draped in numerous robes and veils.
The sun's radiant warmth enveloped him,
expelling the cold from his limbs.
Although he was seemingly dead,
he was revived, causing great astonishment;
the dragon began to awaken from its slumber.

47

When will everyone achieve this goal?
It is essential for a person, like Moses,
to overcome the monster.
The dragon's power led to the defeat and death of so many.

48

Your Self, like a dragon, cannot be fully vanquished,
afflicted by deep sadness and sense of powerlessness.
The dragon is tamed by the snow of detachment;
do not expose it to the allure of earthly indulgence.

49

This teaching is intended for those
who choose to distance themselves from others,
and who lack awareness of the present moment.
Unless a person transcends sensory experience,
they will remain unaware of the concealed, inner truth.

50

The dragon devoured the bewildered person in one gulp,
showing its ability to consume
even the blood of pilgrims with ease.
It coiled around a small bone and
squeezed till it cracked.

Part 6

Youth &
the Desire for Power

51

Monarchs, despite their regal status,
have not truly found the essence of devotion.
If they had, their lack of understanding and wisdom
would have rendered them vulnerable to swift overthrow.
But to preserve the stability of the universe,
God has endowed them with love and devotion,
safeguarding their rule.

52

In the quest for independence,
people may claim to possess godlike attributes.
But the pursuit of collective authority is subject to scrutiny.
While many may revel in shared prosperity,
two forms of leadership cannot coexist.
Such ideals are unsustainable in the physical world,
as those in power seek to eliminate any form of equality
and will ultimately strive to eradicate their competitors.

53

Position grants a shameful privilege to the ignorant.
How could it bestow the prestige of a hundred lions
upon a single person?
Their flaws are concealed, much like a secret instrument;
the serpent reveals itself through a crevice in the desert.
Under the harsh rule of an uneducated king,
the entire desert becomes infested with snakes
and scorpions.

54

Just as prisoners are given titles,
and a person's skin colour may be described
as 'camphor-white',
those ensnared by desire, anger, and misguided optimism
are ultimately defined by their fate,
as though they were kings.

55

According to scholars,
the abyss of darkness has been seized by the oppressors.
The greater the injustice, the harder the downfall.
Justice dictates that the magnitude of punishment increases
in proportion to the scale of injustice.

56

When leadership is entrusted to the misguided,
the leader mistakenly views themself
as holding genuine power,
only ultimately to face the consequences
of their own misguided actions.
Their insufficient expertise and
knowledge lead to destruction.

57

Who, other than you,
O wielder of fire, can speak the truth
only when hidden beneath a blanket?

58

Kings exert their power over their subjects,
turning the wheel of fate into a fine green powder.
A king is like a reservoir,
and each subject, a pipe.
The water flows from the reservoir through the pipes.
If the water in the reservoir is pure,
every pipe will carry clean, sweet water.
But if the water is salty and dirty,
each pipe will deliver water of the same tainted quality.

59

Are you familiar with the phrase,
'The kingdom is infertile'?
It reflects how the king, fearful for his own position,
has severed all ties with his family.

60

Anyone who publicly flaunts their attractiveness
will encounter numerous woes.
They will be stared at,
invite feelings of anger, and a vivid array of colours,
like water pouring from a bottle of musk.
Enemies, driven by jealousy, tear them apart,
and even friends, over time, betray them.

Part 7

Youth & Responsibility

61

How have you allocated your time and energy in your life?
Where have you directed your vitality and focus?
How have you used the precious gift of your vision?
How have you enhanced your five senses?
If you have squandered these invaluable resources
– your sight, hearing, and mind –
what have you truly gained?

62

You have diminished your own worth,
forsaking the revered existence that even angels admired.
Despite your ambitious pursuit of the stars,
you have neglected to recognize
the esteemed position of humanity.

63

The leader of the devils once laid out a path of deception,
strategically setting snares
of unawareness through the night.
When people inadvertently stepped on these thorns,
they expressed their dissatisfaction to him.
But over the centuries, many others followed this path,
unaware of the pitfalls he had placed.

64

If you wish to inspire tears of compassion,
show sympathy towards those who are grieving.
If you seek mercy, extend it to those who are vulnerable.

65

If you are shaped by reality
with an outwardly displeasing appearance,
do not compound this
with an unappealing demeanour
or sour disposition.
Avoid treacherous paths if your shoes are worn;
do not exacerbate existing flaws
if you already face other challenges.

66

Do not shift the blame for your wrongdoings onto others.
Recognize and value your own intelligence
and capacity for reflection.
The responsibility for your actions lies with you,
as you are the one who has committed the mistake.
Seek reconciliation with justice and accept
the consequences set forth by a higher power.

67

Do not attribute your shortcomings to fate.
Why shift the blame for your own failings on to others?
Instead, reflect on your own behaviour
and avoid fixating on the trivial.

68

Whether you face positive or negative outcomes,
they are the result of your own actions.
Both discomfort and contentment arise
from within yourself.
If you suffer from harsh consequences,
it is because you yourself have created them.
Conversely, if you enjoy rich rewards,
it is because you have earned them.

69

He declared his intention to embrace faith,
contingent upon divine will,
and stated that his certainty would depend
on the changing seasons.
But his personal desires and the influence of Satan
led him astray,
causing divine favour to turn into anger
and devastation.

70

Just because you see your own flaws before others do,
does that mean you need no self-improvement?
Those who lack awareness of their own shortcomings
inevitably highlight the imperfections of others.

Part 8

Youth & Friendship

71

There are three types of companions,
if you are aware:
acquaintances for material gain;
acquaintances in speech;
and acquaintances of the spirit.
Provide support to those who reciprocate
with similar support, and then move on.
Show affection to those who respond
with words of friendship.
But it is crucial to value and nurture true friends,
those who connect with your innermost Self.
Show your unwavering devotion to them,
even to the extent of sacrificing your own life, if necessary.

72

Numerous adversaries find satisfaction in your misfortune,
but a companion who empathizes with your grief
is truly essential.

73

If you had the ability to tell enemies from allies,
life would need to be experienced twice.

74

Avoid fools as Jesus did,
for associating with fools leads to problems.
Just as air gradually draws water from the sea,
a foolish person erodes your trust.

75

When hearts are entrusted with sincerity,
this unity enhances your efforts.
One endeavour becomes quadrupled in its purpose,
and four adversaries are unified through harmony.

76

Having a shared language
creates a sense of connection and unity.
Conversely, the inability to communicate with others
can feel restrictive and isolating.
While many Hindus and Turks
speak the same language among themselves,
many Turks remain unfamiliar with one another.

77

I recall receiving wisdom from a knowledgeable elder,
and I urge you to heed this advice:
refrain from wishing for others,
what you do not wish for yourself.

78

My heart is like a shell,
and my friend, the precious pearl inside.
I am overwhelmed with emotion,
as my heart is filled with thoughts of them.

79

My dear friend,
we share a deep bond of companionship.
No matter where you go,
I will always support you and be there for you.

80

My eyes are entirely focused on the image
of my friend's face.
I derive great satisfaction from seeing the world
through these eyes,
as long as my friend remains present.

Part 9

Youth & Learning
From Experience

81

Even the wise are destined to disappear,
serving as a lesson for those who lack understanding.

82

The heart that once inflicted suffering on many
now experiences suffering itself
from the punishment of divine justice.
Fortunate is the person who learns from this experience,
and finds wisdom in these valuable lessons.

83

Those who lack the ability to perceive deeply
will find themselves feeble and devoid of value.

84

You find solace in the night,
yet the day disrupts it.
Extract wisdom from the recurring pattern
of night and day.

85

By observing the experiences of others,
I have gained valuable insights
and transformed myself into someone with keen
perception.
Behold, curious explorer of the world's enigmas,
direct your gaze toward me,
for I have uncovered these profound truths.

86

May the descendants of Adam take heed from Iblis,[3]
who derided Adam and consequently suffered humiliation
in both the earthly realm and the hereafter.

---

3   The leader of the devils, in Islamic tradition.

87

Exercise self-control over your speech,
and enhance your ability to perceive,
as the path to wisdom has already been established
before you.

88

The truly wise individual is the one who gains knowledge
from the loss of friends,
and exercises caution in times of disaster.

89

Suppress your anger,
and widen your perspective.
Experience joy,
gain knowledge from others,
and cultivate wisdom.

90

Fortunate is the individual who retains their heart,
gaining wisdom from the fate of those
who have been removed from power.

Part 10
Youth & Imagination

91

Imagination is intangible,
yet it resides within the mind;
you perceive a world propelled solely by imagination.
Their tranquility and discord arise solely from delusion,
as do their arrogance and embarrassment,
everything grounded in imagination.

92

Every individual enthralled by their own imagination
develops an interest in a valuable goal,
and pursues it with great enthusiasm.
One person may aspire to live in luxury,
influenced by a fictional story,
venturing deep into mountains and mines.
While another, motivated by the same tale,
sets off to the sea in search of precious pearls.

93

In the absence of the genuine form,
it manifests in the realm of imagination,
causing you to become misled.
At times, it creates the illusion of relaxation,
while at others,
it assumes the guise of a commercial enterprise,
a source of wisdom,
or even a place of belonging and kinship.

94

Many instances of cruelty that you observe in others
may, in fact, reflect your own character.
The traits of deceit, unfairness, and folly
that you perceive in them
are actually reflections of your own behaviour.
The wounds you recognize are caused by your own actions,
and in truth, you are only condemning yourself.

95

A mind that is divided,
troubled by imagination and distrust,
finds itself in a state of darkness.
A brief pathway on the ground becomes hazardous,
while a tall wall appears dangerous
when your mind is troubled.

96

All of this is a product of your imagination.
Truly, I harbour no resentment towards you.
Do not view me
through the filter of your negative thoughts.
Why do you nurture doubt
towards those who have affection for you?

97

Imagination acts as a vigilant sentinel,
armed with a spear,
forming a protective barrier around the sanctuary
of beauty and truth,
preventing any intruder from gaining access.
Whenever a person seeking something approaches,
their ability to think creatively takes control,
preventing them from making any progress.

98

Every day, the soul is oppressed
by the burden of imagination,
consumed by concerns
of acquiring, losing, and the dread of deterioration.
This unwavering focus leaves no room
for clarity, elegance,
or the journey towards spiritual enlightenment.

99

These groups have succumbed
to the profound deceptions of the material world,
with each person wrongly perceiving
their own self-image as the ultimate truth.
If a person is unable to distinguish their own nature
from the numerous illusions
and fantasies that surround them,
and instead builds their life path around these fallacies,
they will perpetually remain far from their true position.

100

Beautiful imaginations are shaped moment by moment,
emerging from nothingness
in direct proportion to every thought.

Finis

www.ingramcontent.com/pod-product-compliance
Lightning Source LLC
Chambersburg PA
CBHW020451100426
42813CB00031B/3327/J